Stop Dreaming &

Start Doing

A Practical Guide for Getting What You Want
With SMART Goals

KAHOKA PRESS

ISBN: 978-0-692-22337-6

Published in the United States by Kahoka Press

About the Author

Annette Richmond, MA is a writer, optimist, media enthusiast and executive editor of career-intelligence.com. Having changed careers several times, including working as a career coach, she has a unique perspective on career management. When starting career-intelligence.com over a decade ago, her goal was to provide a one-stop online career resource.

In addition to being a writer, speaker and consultant, Richmond contributes career-related articles to various other sites including ForbesWoman. She holds a BA in English from Sacred Heart University and a MA in Applied Psychology from Fairfield University. She resides in Rowayton, CT, with her husband, Eric, and their four-legged kids

For timely, relevant career information and advice follow her on Twitter @careerintell and visit career-intelligence.com.

Table of Contents

Planning: What's Your Style? 9

What Are Goals? 17

Getting Started: What do you want? 21

Goals: The Long & Short Of It 25

Are You Setting SMART Goals? 31

Creating Your Action Plan 37

Don't Let Fear Stop You 45

Developing A Support System 51

Cheerleaders & Others 57

Putting It All Together 61

Are You Ready? Let's Go 67

Goals Worksheet 72

Table of Contents

If you want a place in the sun, prepare to put up with a few blisters.

~ Abigail Van Buren (Dear Abby)

I've missed more than 9,000 shots in my career. I've lost almost 300 games; 26 times I've been trusted to take the game-winning shot and missed. I've failed over and over and over again in my life. And that is why I succeed.

~ Michael Jordan

Life's a bitch. You've got to go out and kick ass.

~ Maya Angelou

Planning: What's Your Style?

By failing to prepare, you are preparing to fail.
> ~ Benjamin Franklin

Are you a born planner? If you're a planner you know it. As soon as you decide to do something, whether it's going on vacation or buying a new car, you begin to plan. Maybe you go online to search for vacation deals. If you're buying a car, you may schedule some time to visit auto dealerships. Once you've decided what you want to accomplish, you focus on making it happen.

For some of us this is a natural process. For some of us it's not.

I'm not a born planner. All through high-school and college I waited until the last minute to get things done. The weekend before a paper was due, I started writing it. I didn't bother to create an outline; I just sat down and started putting words on paper. Fact was, I enjoyed the little rush working last minute to meet a deadline gave me. And most of the time this process worked for me.

Once I began writing professionally the expectations people had of me were higher. Now that writing was my job "most of the time" wasn't good enough. After my first month or so as an assistant editor, I was responsible for writing a few columns. I needed to arrange phone interviews and prepare questions in advance. Everyday I was working on several different projects. At certain times of the year, we were writing and editing two issues of the magazine at the same time. I was overwhelmed.

Luckily, I had Villia. She was a great editor who taught me how to work on at least somewhat of a schedule. For the first several months, she gave me incremental deadlines to help me stay on track. Under her guidance I began to work more productively and meet my deadlines without being breathless at the finish line. She taught me the value of having time for finishing touches. She taught me to know when it was time to finish a project and move on. She taught me to be a professional writer.

A few years later, I learned how to take planning a step further. After spending several years at the magazine and some time as a freelance writer, I decided it was time for a career change. So I returned to school.

In 1998, I was completing a master's degree in applied psychology program. Much to my amazement before I graduated I had my first job in the field: I was hired as a vocational counselor at a non-profit training and placement facility.

As a vocational counselor one of the biggest parts of my job would be helping my clients set their goals. Something I wasn't very good at, at least not yet. Fortunately, the agency provided training designed to teach the staff effective goal-setting techniques. We, in turn, would pass the techniques on to our clients.

When I was working with clients our goal-setting process went something like this. First, I helped my client figure out what he or she wanted to do in their next position. Most of my clients wanted to work in some type of administrative job. This was their long-term goal.

Once the client's long-term goal was established, we worked together on a plan to help them get there. Most often, the plan included computer training and lessons in office skills. At the end of the training another counselor helped them with job placement. Since most of our clients wanted to work in an administrative role, nearly everyone needed to increase their typing speed. This was a short-term goal.

But, "type faster" was not concrete enough. It wasn't something that could be measured. So we concentrated on setting SMART goals (Specific, Measurable, Achievable, Realistic and Time-framed). A SMART goal, for example, might be for someone to increase their typing speed from 25 to 55 words per minute in two-months. Their daily activities would include 30-minutes of practice typing. We would measure their progress with a weekly typing test. Not very exciting stuff, but it was effective.

When I saw how much setting goals helped my clients, I started to use the process in my own life. And guess what, it worked. But it wasn't easy.

As I said, I'm not a born planner. Everything in my being wants to just go with the flow and see what happens. Wait until the last minute whenever possible. But I never understood why I embraced this behavior which often worked against me.

Several years later when I was going through training to administer the Myers-Briggs Type Indicator® – commonly known as the MBTI® – I discovered that I was kind of "hard-wired" to resist planning.

If you're not familiar with the MBTI it's one of the most widely used instruments in the world. Developed by Isabel Briggs Myers and her mother Katherine Cook Briggs, the Indicator is designed to help people discover their preferences and tendencies on four dichotomous, or opposite, scales: how we take in data and give it meaning; how we make decisions, judgments and take action; where our source of personal energy comes from; and how we prefer to interact with the external world.

The last scale – the Judging/Perceiving Dichotomy – reveals our preferences, or preferred ways of dealing with the world, particularly when it comes to making plans. Here are a few characteristics of each.

Those who prefer Judging

> Are systematic and methodical
> Like to organize their lives
> Make short- and long-term plans
> Are more comfortable when things are decided
> Try to avoid last-minute stress

Those who prefer Perceiving

> Are spontaneous and flexible
> Like to "go with the flow"
> Avoid making plans
> Prefer to keep their options open
> Feel energized by last-minute stress

Studying and then taking the MBTI myself was a real eye-opener in many ways, it helped be understand myself and others in many areas. But here I'm just going to focus on the fourth scale - Judging/Perceiving. My results indicated a strong preference for Perceiving.

No wonder I had trouble making plans.

But the MBTI only indicates preferences. While we may have preference for doing things one way sometimes that preference can get in our way.

Being someone who liked to "go with the flow" wasn't an asset when I wanted to accomplish something in my personal or professional life. For example, being spontaneous, which often meant pizza for dinner, didn't help when I wanted to drop 20 pounds. Making changes required a plan.

When I forced myself to think seriously about my goals something great happened. I was forced to come up with ideas for reaching my objectives. Setting long-term goals gave me something concrete to strive for. Short-term goals provided the steps to get me there and made my main objectives seem less overwhelming. Daily activities provided a foundation. The bonus was that having a plan helped me stay focused.

Now it's my turn to share this process with you. In this book, you'll find step-by-step instructions for creating your plan. You'll be in charge of setting your own long-term goals. You'll be the one figuring out what you need to do, the steps you need to take and setting a time frame for doing it. But, I'll use concrete examples to explain how.

Even if you're a born planner, chances are you haven't been working as effectively as you might be. Have you been setting yourself up for failure with unrealistic expectations? Do you get disheartened and give up when you don't make a lot of progress right away? Don't let that discourage you. All you need is a little training.

You'll find that effective goal setting can help turn your dreams into reality.

16

What Are Goals?

A goal without a plan is just a wish.

~ Antoine de Saint-Exupéry

Ever make a New Year's resolution? If you answered yes, you're just like the rest of us. It's one of our collective favorite pastimes. There's something about a brand new calendar that suggests the opportunity to start all over again.

Whether your New Year's resolution was to find a new job, get a promotion, market your business more successfully or to make more time for yourself, you'll get more results if you set some concrete goals. Yes, goals.

Think about it. How many times have you promised yourself that you would "eat healthier" or "exercise regularly" or "whatever?" And how many times have you followed-through? If the answer is "not often," I'm guessing that you probably didn't write down specific goals.

That's OK. Each beginning of a new year, start of a new month or dawn of a new day, offers another chance to make a fresh start. The key to turning your resolutions into results is to make a plan. Create one that includes long- and short-term goals, daily activities, and plenty of opportunities to measure your achievements along the way.

Remember when you were in school? When you started first grade you weren't thinking about graduating from college, or even getting into junior high school. Sure, somewhere in the back of your head you knew those were your final objectives. But, when you started first grade your long-term goal was to pass with the rest of your class, to make it to second grade.

On the first day of class your main objective was to figure out what was expected of you. Once you learned the ground rules, your focus was a series of short-term goals: passing your first test, making new friends, getting through the first semester, passing your final exams, then moving on to the second grade.

Whatever you want to do, your strategy should be the same: set up long-term goals, short-term goals, and concentrate on overcoming them one hurdle at a time. Maybe today is the day you decide to adopt a "healthier lifestyle." This is a common resolution. Often prompted by a run up the stairs that left you gasping for air or a day spent shopping for bathing suits. But where should you start? Begin by determining what you really want to achieve.

OK, let's start getting specific.

What is your vision of success? Everyone holds a different image in his or her mind. For one person it's having the corner office, for another it's having a flexible schedule with plenty of time off to be with his or her kids. Still others want to run their own business.

What have you been daydreaming about? What have you been putting off because it seems overwhelming and you don't know where to start? Whatever your dream, setting effective goals will help you make it come true.

Spend a little time thinking about it now. In the next chapter, we'll go over how to create a plan. It will include a detailed example of how to set long-term goals, short-term goals and daily activities.

Getting Started: What do you want?

If you don't know where you are going, you'll end up someplace else.

~ *Yogi Berra*

What do you want? The first step in the process is to figure out your long-term goals. These are not generalizations like "get into shape" or "increase my business". These are specific statements of what you intend to do. You probably will have several goals for both your personal and professional lives.

Let's look at an example. Whether your goal is to find a new job or increase your business, networking should be part of your plan. But, "networking" in and of itself is too vague to be a goal.

After my first year as an entrepreneur I decided I wanted to increase my business by building my connections. To be more specific, I wanted to create a network of people with similar values that I could rely on for information, introductions and support.

Now, I love the flexibility of working from home. Unfortunately, one of the down sides of a home office is that you tend to become isolated. Since these were the days before social media I knew that if building a network was one of my goals, I needed to get out of my sweats, and actually leave my house to meet people.

My short-term goal was to find a few local organizations where I could meet people and make connections. But, where would I start? Fortunately, I met someone who gave me a few ideas of where to begin. She told me about two local organizations: the Entrepreneurial Women's Network (EWN), where I would have the opportunity to meet other small business owners like me, and Fairfield Network of Executive Women (FNEW), where I could touch base with women who were in corporate life.

The following month, I visited both groups. From the women I met at those events I learned about other organizations that might be good matches for me. At the end of three months, I had visited five different groups and selected two that seemed to best suit my current needs. I choose the two that I felt offered the best opportunities to make connections and provided the right venues for meeting people who could help move me toward my goal of increasing my business.

Now I knew where to find people. I was ready to move on to another short-term goal. I decided I wanted to connect with two to three new people each month. Because I worked primarily on the web, I set my sites on meeting two people offline and one person online.

OK, let's take another look at my long-term goal. I want to create a network of people with similar values that I can rely on for information, introductions and support. To achieve this goal I needed to set several short-term goals: find places to network, determine which organizations would help me meet the types of people I was looking for and set a monthly number of how many people I wanted to meet. And, because this was all new to me, I needed to add another short-term goal: To develop better networking skills.

If the idea of meeting new people makes you weak in the knees, learn how to do it better. At another colleague's suggestion, I picked up copies of Susan RoAne's *How to Work a Room? The Ultimate Guide To Savvy Socializing In Person And Online* and *The Secrets of Savvy Networking: How To Make The Best Connections For Business and Personal Success*. Both are packed with information and entertaining anecdotes that will help you prepare for any networking event. (A revised 25th Anniversary edition of *How to Work a Room*, published in 2014, is now available in paperback and on Kindle.)

Is building a network one of your goals? Then determine what it will take for you to reach it. Experiment with different organizations and venues to determine which work best for you.

To review, once I developed my long-term goal of networking - to create a network of people with similar values that I could rely on for information, introductions and support – I developed several short-term goals 1) Find places to network, 2) Attend a fixed amount of networking events 3) Develop better networking skills, and 4) Connect with a certain number of people each month..

These are the basics of goal setting. In the next chapter we'll go over specific examples of long- and short-term goals.

Goals: The Long & Short Of It

Actions speak louder than words.

~ Dale Carnegie

By now you know that setting goals is more than making vague statements like, "I will find a new job" or "I will lose some weight." It means creating a written plan that includes reasonable and measurable long-term and short-term objectives.

Because nearly everyone can relate to getting in shape, I'm going to use weight loss to illustrate the goal-setting process. Let's say, you want to drop a few pounds. That's a common resolution on New Year's Eve and one month before bathing-suit season begins. The first step is to figure out how much weight you'd like to lose and how quickly you want to lose it. Remember your goals need to be reasonable, as well as measurable: It's unlikely you'll lose ten pounds in one week without surgery.

To explain the process, I'll use myself as an example. There came a day when I decided that I needed to lose a few pounds. Actually, it was more that I could no longer rationalize that those extra pounds were water weight. As I was getting dressed for a luncheon I discovered that my suit was too small. It wasn't only that my slacks felt like they were strangling me, the zipper simply refused to budge. While it probably sounds funny to read about it now, back then it wasn't amusing.

After considerable thought - which included evaluating the clothes in my closet - I decided I needed to lose 15 pounds. That was my long-term goal. Now I needed to figure out how to make it happen.

OK, where would I start? My first stop was the Internet. Happily I found many credible health sites with good information. Research told me that healthy weight loss was approximately one-to-two pounds per week. So I decided that I would lose 15 pounds in four months: at one-to-two pounds per week this was a reasonable expectation. Because I wanted to tone up as well, I decided to include exercise as well as diet in my weight-loss plan.

Now I was ready to set my short-term goals. These would be the steps I'd take to achieve my long-term objective: lose 15 pounds in four months. From experience, I knew that having daily and weekly goals would be the best way for me to track my progress. Since I'm easily distracted, I also knew things like daily goals would help me stay focused. Using these principles, here's the weight-loss plan I developed.

My Weight Loss Plan

Long-term Goal: Lose fifteen pounds in four months

Short-term Goals

Monthly

> Lose four to six pounds each month
>
> Eat an overall healthy diet, cut sweets to a minimum
>
> Exercise regularly, include aerobic workouts and weight training
>
> Determine Progress – at the end of each month I would compare my weight and body measurements to those of the previous month. Also, calculate how many days I met my exercise and nutrition goals.

Weekly

> Lose one-to-two pounds a week
>
> Write down my weight and body measurements at the end of each week.

Review my exercise log to see how many days I met my exercise goals and look through my food diary to see how much food I consumed each day.

Exercise: aerobic exercise 30 to 45 minutes five or six times each week to burn fat, weight training for 20 to 30 minutes Monday, Wednesday and Friday each week, abdominal exercises five or six times a week to help tone my stomach.

Determine Progress – compare my weight and body measurements to those of the previous week Also, see how many days I met my exercise and nutrition goals.

Daily Activities

Eat a healthy diet: protein shake or cereal for breakfast, sensible lunch and dinner

Keep a food diary (I will keep track of my food intake by writing down everything I eat.)

Drink six to eight glasses of water a day (I will write this down in my food diary.)

Complete my daily exercises (I will keep track of my program by writing down my daily exercise.)

Both my long-term and short-term goals were reasonable and measurable. Each time I exercised I made a notation in my weight-loss notebook. Making note of when I exercised and keeping a food diary helped me monitor my activities. Knowing that I was keeping track of what I ate and how often I exercised made me accountable. I was less likely to eat that donut if I had to write it in my food diary at the end of the day. Every day I knew that I was working towards my long-term goal. And, yes, at the end of four months I lost 15 pounds.

Getting into shape may or may not be one of your goals. However you can use the same principles to create your plan. Let's say you want to find a new job and you think it will take you six months to a year. Your long-term goal is to find a new job in six months to a year. Your short-term goals might include:

Researching opportunities within your current company

Developing a list of target companies (companies you'd like to work for)

Updating your current resume or better yet creating a new one

Updating your social media presence, create a LinkedIn profile if you don't already have one

Talking to your friends and family (making them aware that you're looking and asking for help)

Exploring other possible careers (doing research and conducting informational interviews, etc.)

Enhancing your communication skills (maybe joining Toastmasters)

Gaining new experience with temporary positions (if you're not already working) and/or volunteer opportunities

Getting some additional training (picking up new computer skill, etc.)

You'll need to develop a plan based on your situation. Just make sure your daily activities help you achieve your short-term goals and they, in turn, move you towards your long-term objective. Because our objectives often change with time it's also important to continually review your goals.

Generally speaking, long-term goals are objectives that will take at least six-to-twelve months to reach. Short-term goals should be no longer than one-to-three months. But, you'll be more effective if you have weekly goals – or mini-goals - too. Otherwise it can take too long to see progress. When setting your short-term goals be sure to include plenty of opportunities for success along the way.

Take some time to write down your current goals. In the next chapter, we'll talk about how to make your goals more effective.

Are You Setting SMART Goals?

Never confuse movement with action.

~ Ernest Hemingway

If you want your goal-setting process to be effective, you need to develop concrete, measurable goals. In the last chapter, we looked at the technique of setting long- and short-term goals. Here we'll refine the goal-setting process even more.

Lots of counselors and coaches use the SMART acronym to explain the finer points of goal setting. Each one uses a slightly different set of criteria. In this explanation, SMART refers to goals that are **S**pecific, **M**easurable, **A**chievable, **R**ealistic and **T**ime-Framed.

Specific: Goals need to be concrete. Often we set goals that are so loose, it's nearly impossible to judge whether we hit them or not. For example, a statement like "I will lose weight" is too vague.

Ask yourself these questions: How much weight will you lose? What is your target date? How will you know if and when you've reached your goal? Saying, " I will lose five pounds in one month" is more specific. At the end of the month it will be a simple matter of weights and measures to gage your progress: take your measurements and get on the scale.

Measurable: Goals need to be quantifiable. For example, whatever we do for a living, most of us want to increase our business network. But, "making new contacts" is an ambiguous statement. Where will we meet new people? How many people can we reasonably expect to meet in a month?

A clearer objective might be "I will attend four networking events each month and try to connect with one likeminded person at each." It's a simple, concrete goal. At the end of the month it will be easy to see if you hit your target.

Achievable: Goals need to be reasonable and achievable. Like me, nearly everyone has tried to drop a few pounds at one time or another. Often their success or failure depends on setting practical goals.

Unfortunately, people often set goals based on unreasonable expectations. Losing 15 pounds in 30 days is unrealistic (unless you're planning a medical procedure or an unhealthy diet). Losing four to six pounds in 30 days is considered healthy weight-loss. Don't set yourself up for failure by setting goals that are out of reach.

Realistic: Goals need to be realistic for you. When we're kids we think we can do anything. As adults we learn that while we can have a lot, we can't have it all at the same time. It's important to honestly evaluate your options.

Do you have the ability and commitment to make your dream come true? Or does it need a little adjustment? For example, you may love to play tennis, but do you have the time, talent and commitment to become a pro? Be honest. Particularly about the commitment.

Time Framed: Goals need to have some kind of target date. Your target date might be one year from now. It might be five years. But, without a time frame, it's still a daydream. Which is fine, as long as you know the difference.

Having a set amount of time will give your goals structure. For example, many of us want to find a new job or start our own business. Some people spend a lot of time talking about what they want to do, someday. But, without an end date there is no sense of urgency, no reason to take any action today. Having a specific time frame gives you the impetus to get started. It also helps you monitor your progress.

Why are SMART goals so effective? Each component of the SMART acronym has some of the elements of working with a personal coach.

Specific goals – keep you focused on your activities, help you decide what you need to do next

Measurable goals – provide you with constant feedback, if you're trying to lose weight the scale will let you know how you're doing

Achievable – keep you motivated, little successes will help you hang in there for the long haul

Realistic – keeps you energized, knowing you can reach your goals is half the battle

Time-framed – creates a sense of urgency, forces you to create a plan

Setting goals is more than deciding what you want to do. It involves figuring out what you need to do to get where you want to go and how long it will take you to get there. Writing down your goals is important. But, before you set your pen to paper, take a minute to think about your objectives. Remember the SMART acronym: Make sure your goals are:

Specific – is this something concrete?

Measurable – can it be measured by anyone?

Achievable – is this within my reach?

Realistic – do research and reason indicate this can be done?

Time-framed – is there target date?

If you answered yes to all of these questions, you've set effective goals. You're on your way to achieving your objectives.

Now you know the fundamentals. You know the importance of setting long- and short-term goals. You know how to develop a step-by-step plan. Keeping the SMART acronym in mind will help you remember the basics. Each time you write down a goal, spend some time to think about it. Soon setting effective goals will become second nature.

In the next chapter, Creating Your Action Plan, we'll translate the effective goal-setting process to fit your needs. Get ready for some serious thinking.

Creating Your Action Plan

*An ant on the move does more
than a dozing ox.*

~ Lao-Tzu

Now you know the basics. You know the importance of
setting long-term and short-term goals. You know how to set
Specific, **M**easurable, **A**chievable, **R**ealistic and **T**ime
Framed goals. So let's get started.

Setting a long-term goal

OK, pick one thing you want to accomplish in the next six
months to a year, or longer. Is it to get into shape? Find a
new job? Or maybe start your own business?

Whatever your goal, you need to start with a concrete
statement of your objective. Once you've formulated your
goal, write it down. (Remember my weight loss example I will
lose 15 pounds in four months.)

37

_____

_____

_____

_____

_____

Now, you have your long-term objective, you're ready to move on to the next step: setting short-term goals.

Your short-term goals

Congratulations! You've set one of your long-term goals. The next step is to figure out what it will take for you to reach your objective.

Take another look at your long-term goal. Now take some time to write down a few short-term goals. Remember the SMART acronym: Make sure your goals are:

Specific – is this something concrete?

Measurable – can it be measured by anyone?

Achievable – is this within my reach?

Realistic – do research and reason indicate this can be done?

Time Framed – is there a target date?

Let's say your long-term goal will take six months to reach. You will need to set at least monthly and weekly objectives. When I planned to lose 15 pounds in four months, for example, I set monthly goals of four to six pounds and weekly weight loss of one to two pounds.

While my exercise and nutrition requirements were designed to help me meet my weekly and monthly goals, they also helped keep me focused. Every day I felt a sense of accomplishment when I finished exercising or looked in my food diary to see that I hadn't eaten any sweets that day.

Remember to incorporate opportunities for success into your program.

Monthly Goals:

1._____

2_____

3._____

(Make sure to include how you will measure your progress.)

Weekly Goals:

1._____

2._____

3._____

4._____

(Make sure to include how you will measure your progress.)

Daily Activities: These are things you will do on a daily basis that will help you move towards your long- and short-term goals. You might want to include activities such as positive thinking, reading, talking to your partner for support. Anything and everything that will help you move in the right direction.

1._____

2._____

3._____

4._____

5._____

Staying Motivated

The first few days, or even weeks, it's easy to stay with your Action Plan. But, after the initial excitement has worn off you'll need to help yourself stay motivated.

If your long-term goal is losing weight maybe you plan to buy a new pair of jeans once you reach your goal of losing 20 pounds. But, six months is a long time to wait. Even two months can seem like an eternity.

Remember when you were a kid? Did your parents wait to reward you for reading until you were reading Shakespeare? I didn't think so. I bet they took you out for ice-cream when you were able to read three-word sentences. Well you need to reward yourself too. Although if you're losing weight not with ice-cream.

And don't wait until you've lost 10 pounds. Create mini-goals along the way. There are endless options. You might choose to give yourself a treat after you've followed your healthy diet for one week or reward yourself for sticking to the exercise program you've created for two weeks. A treat doesn't have to be something big, just something that's a treat for you.

If you're trying to lose weight you know that reward probably doesn't mean a donut for breakfast. But, what about going to see the movie everyone is talking about? Or maybe treating yourself to a guilt-free afternoon of watching DVD's or maybe a ball game?

Once you've lost five pounds buy yourself the CD or DVD you've been wanting. Get two when you've lost 10 pounds. Giving yourself rewards along the way helps to keep you motivated.

Now you have all the elements to create your Action Plan. You'll find that the more you use the goal-setting process, the easier it will become. Before you finish putting together your plan here are a few more things to think about.

First, it's important to always write down your goals. Writing them down helps with the process. There's also something about writing things down that makes them more "real." Buy a notebook in your favorite color for inspiration. To keep your goals in sight get a supersized Post-It® Table-top pad that you can stick on any wall.

Second, talk about your goals to others. For one thing, you never know who might be able to help you along your way. Also, there's nothing like telling your best friend you're going to drop ten pounds to make you feel accountable.

Third, use your family and friends for emotional support. Find at least one ally who will applaud your successes. And encourage you when you miss the mark.

Once you've formulated your plan for success – whatever you determine that to be – make sure you review your goals at least every few months. Times change, and we change with them. What we want today, we may not want tomorrow. And the most important thing about your goals is that they be yours.

While I know that creating lists works for some people, I know that others are more visual. For more visual thinkers I've created an Action Plan flow-chart.

Action Plan

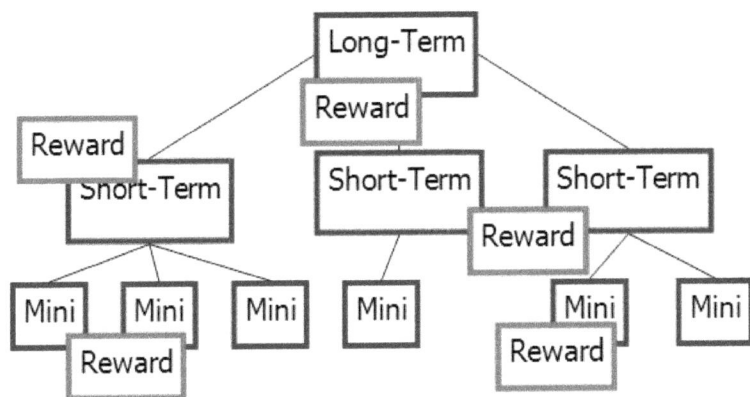

Don't Let Fear Stop You

*And the trouble is, if you don't risk
anything, you risk even more.*

~ Erica Jong

Nearly everyone I know is afraid of doing something. If
they're not afraid of anything right now, at one time or
another they have been. While the thing that gives you
butterflies in your stomach may not be the same thing that
makes me weak in the knees, there is always something. For
some of us it's giving a speech. For others it's exchanging
the security of one job for the uncertainness of a new
position. Unfortunately, our fears can stop us from moving
forward, if we let them.

What about you? What are you afraid of? What fears are
keeping you from achieving your dreams? Are you stuck in a
job rut because you're afraid that you won't be able to find
something else? Do you avoid networking events because

you're scared to go by yourself? Are you unable to increase your business because you're afraid of rejection?

Don't get discouraged, at one time or another everyone else has been afraid too.

Earlier I talked about my goal of building a bigger network. To be more specific: I wanted to create a network of people with similar values that I could rely on for information, introductions and support to increase my business.

I also mentioned that a colleague gave me the names of a few organizations to start with. I should have been off and running. The problem was that I was afraid. As a writer, I was used to interviewing people both in person and over-the-phone, everyone from company presidents to department store buyers to small business owners. I met hundreds of people when I was covering trade shows. But, that was different. It was never about me, it was always about the story.

Now, the spotlight was turned on me. I was a newbie entrepreneur trying to sell my business and myself to strangers. To make things worst many of the women I met were already quite successful. I was worried about what I would do, what I would say and most importantly, what they would think of me.

Although, I knew my goal was to meet people, I often went to events a little late and hung out in the corner. If someone talked to me, I was friendly. But, I usually didn't initiate conversations. And I dreaded every event.

Well, as Susan Jeffers says in *Feel the Fear and Do It Anyway* the only way to conquer your fear is to do whatever it is you're afraid of. Yes, things like positive self-talk and changing your attitude will increase your self-confidence. Which is a good thing as far as it goes. But, the only way to move past your fear is to take action.

And that's what I finally did. I asked a few successful women for advice. I looked for events where the speaker's topic was networking. In the course of one week, two people recommended Susan RoAne's *The Secrets of Savvy Networking*. The second time someone mentioned her book I went out and picked up a copy. It looked so intriguing I bought her first book, *How To Work A Room*, as well. AS I mentioned earlier, I read them both. By the time next month's events rolled around, I felt different. I was still nervous, but I felt ready.

Taking a lesson from RoAne, I spent some time preparing for the next EWN luncheon. That day I read the local newspaper and watched some morning television looking for a few interesting things I could talk about. I made it a point to arrive, ready to talk about three different topics. I saw someone standing alone and went up and extended my hand. It wasn't nearly as difficult as I thought it would be.

In *Feel the Fear and Do It Anyway*, Jeffers spends a lot of time talking about our inner chatterbox. It's that insidious voice in your head that tries to make you feel inadequate, assuring you that whatever you do will be wrong. If you're anything like me, yours roars the loudest at the most inopportune times. Don't let that voice stop you from moving forward. The more you step outside of your comfort zone, the less you'll hear from your inner critic.

Now, much to my husband's surprise I actually look forward to networking events. Each one is an adventure. No, I don't meet someone I have a real connection with every time. But, I have met a few likeminded people along the way. And I've enjoyed myself in the process.

What's holding you back? Lots of us are afraid of rejection. Whether that means making those sales calls or contacting someone who can help you get another job. Well, a couple of months ago, I came across a new way of looking at rejection in *The One Minute Manager*, by Kenneth Blanchard, Ph.D. and Spencer Johnson, M.D.

Now, *The One Minute Manager* is a great book, even if the only person you're managing is you. But, my favorite part is in the *Third Secret: One Minute Reprimands*. In this chapter, one of the characters introduces an unusual philosophy: Win or Break Even. All of our lives we learn that when we ask for something we either win or lose. If we get what we want, we win. If we don't, we lose. But, here the thinking is that we either Win or Break Even. If we get what we want we Win. If we don't we're no worse off than before, we Break Even.

Wow, what a concept. Having been raised on the idea of either win or lose, the thought of winning or breaking even was a revelation. Whenever I have to make a tough phone call, I try to remember, if I get what I'm looking for I win, if I don't I break even. Keeping that thought in my mind often helps.

While the only way to truly overcome what you're afraid of is to do it, in my experience being prepared certainly helps. Experiment until you find what will help you do whatever it is you're afraid of doing. And then use it.

There are many good books on the market. My favorites are the ones that entertain while they educate. Ask friends and colleagues for book recommendations until you find one that addresses your concerns.

Who Moved My Cheese? by Spencer Johnson, MD, can help you cope with change in every area of your life. *How To Work A Room* can help you become more comfortable meeting new people. *Never Let'Em See You Sweat*, by Phil Slott, can help you get over any public speaking jitters. (While all of these books have been around for a while their messages are still every bit as relevant today. The other good news is that most are now available on Kindle.)

Whatever is stopping you from moving forward reading *Feel the Fear and Do It Anyway* can give you a few ideas on how to get unstuck. But, that's just the first step to getting what you want. Ultimately it's up to you.

Developing A Support System

I get by with a little help from my friends.

~ John Lennon and Paul McCartney

Most people start off with a lot of enthusiasm. It's easy to stick to a healthy diet, look for a new job, abide by a budget, go to the gym, etc. – in the beginning. It's staying with your plan for more than a month or so that takes determination.

One of the best ways to ensure your success is to develop a support system. Talking to your best friend can be helpful. However, meeting regularly with one or more like-minded people can be invaluable.

Think about it. What do the most successful weight-loss programs like Weight Watchers have in common? Why are groups like Alcoholics Anonymous so successful? Why can working with a coach be more effective than going it alone? It's simple. Each provides you with a support system.

A support system will give you encouragement when things aren't going well, help you create new strategies when you need them, hold you accountable to do what you say you'll do and celebrate your achievements along the way. It can mean the difference between success and failure.

One of the ways to do this is by working with a buddy. If you ever went swimming as a kid you probably remember the buddy-system. The camp counselors would pair each child with another child. When you went swimming your buddy went with you. It was a great way to make sure that everyone stayed safe.

Even though you're not a kid anymore, the buddy system can still be useful. When I quit smoking I did it with a buddy. And having someone who understood exactly what I was going through helped me considerably. But, you don't necessarily have to be working toward the exact same goal as your buddy as long as you are both working on something.

The essential component is the commitment to be there for each other. Each person is there to help the other one to cheer them on, hold them accountable and help them come up with new ideas when it's time to adjust their Action Plan. In Barbara Sher's book *Wishcraft* she suggests meeting with your buddy for a set time on a weekly basis to share encouragement and ideas. She also recommends setting a timer so that each person will have equal time. Smart phones make this easy.

These are some guidelines for holding a 45-minute Buddy Strategy Session.

First 5 minutes - socializing

Next 20 minutes (first person)

> 5 minutes to talk about their successes and failure since the last meeting

> 10 minutes for discussion, to exchange ideas, get encouragement, etc.

> 5 minutes to state what they will do before the next meeting

Final 20 minutes (second person)

> 5 minutes to talk about their successes and failure since the last meeting

> 10 minutes for discussion, to exchange ideas, get encouragement, etc.

> 5 minutes to state what they will do before the next meeting

Time spent – 45 minutes

These sessions can be done in person, over the phone or via a video option like Skype. The important thing is to do it.

While having a Strategy Session with another person can be quite constructive you might find working with a larger group to be more beneficial.

In *Think & Grow Rich* Napoleon Hill explains the power you can unleash with a Mastermind group. A Mastermind being a group of people with similar values and a variety of abilities who can, and will, work together to help each other reach his or her goals. To keep things manageable you'll probably want to keep this to a group of six to eight people.

Now, starting a Mastermind Group is not as easy as finding a buddy. But, it can be done. Someone I know got her first group going by inviting fifteen friends and colleagues over for a business/social get together. Several people came to the first meeting. Over the next few weeks they evolved into a group of six. Although some of the members have changed over time, when I met her the group had been working together for over ten years.

These are some guidelines for holding a two-hour Mastermind Strategy Session.

First 5 - 10 minutes - socializing

Once the meeting begins each person gets 18 minutes

5 minutes to talk about their successes and failure since the last meeting

10 minutes for discussion, to exchange ideas, get encouragement, etc.

3 minutes to state what they will do before the next meeting

Last 5- 10 minutes – wrap up

Time spent – 120 minutes – 2 hours

The last 5 – 10 minutes should be used to discuss Group business such as arranging the next meeting time, discussing potential new members, etc.

On a personal note, I belonged to a Mastermind Group for two years. While the group eventually disbanded, it was truly a valuable resource for me at the time. I continued to meet regularly with one of the other members, although on a less formal basis, for several additional years.

Cheerleaders & Others

You cannot achieve great success until you are faithful to yourself.
> ~ *Friedrich W. Nietzsche*

People are resistant to change. Our instinct tells us not to upset the status quo. Even if the change will be good for us. For the most part, even if we're unhappy with the way things are it's easier, and often more comfortable, to let them stay that way.

By now, you should be ready to embrace the changes in your life. (If you're not feeling ready, go back and reread Don't Let Fear Stop You.) In this chapter we're going to discuss the reactions you may get from the other people in your circle.

While you may expect nothing but support, the fact is that people even resist change in other people's lives. Their biggest concern is how changes in your life will affect them.

I remember when I was in college. I was what is called a non-traditional student. That's someone who doesn't go to college right after high school which is considered the traditional route. That's true even today.

You see I was a college drop-out. Like a lot of kids, I started college the fall after I graduated from high school. However, at the time I was more interested in staying out late with my new boyfriend than in getting up and going to class. I left school before completing even one semester. A few weeks later I was working full-time at a bank.

After several years of assorted jobs, many in restaurants, I decided that I needed to go back to school and start thinking about a career. At the time I was in my twenties, working full-time and living on my own. My life was full and busy.

It had been about ten years since I sat in a classroom. I was nervous and excited all at the same time. My friends, on the other hand, were only nervous. They were worried about how getting a college degree would change me.

My friends were concerned that going to college would make me different. They worried that changes in me would damage our friendship. My girlfriends were annoyed when I couldn't go out or I had to go home early. My boyfriend resented the time I spent studying instead of watching football with him. Much to my surprise, no one was happy with me.

The truth is that I did change. Much of my free time was given to going to class and writing papers. I couldn't stay out till 3 am on Friday night because I needed to be fresh on Saturdays to study. I did well in school and this gave me more confidence in myself. These factors, and more, did affect some of my relationships.

As I changed, I drifted away from some of my old friends. Not surprisingly, my romantic relationship didn't last either. However, the people who were my closest friends are still among my friends today.

Getting my degree is still one of my greatest accomplishments. It took lots of time and dedication. But, it helped me realize that I really do have control over my life. That I could take charge and get what I wanted.

My story is not unusual. Once you decide to make changes in your life you should expect resistance from those that you love. It's not that they don't want you to be happy. It's not that they want to see you fail. Remember they are afraid of two things: how the process will affect their life and how the change will affect their relationship with you.

If, like me, you decide to go back to school how will it affect your family? Will your husband be responsible for getting dinner several nights a week? Will the kids have to share some of the housework?

If you get a new job will you be working late and maybe traveling? How will this cut into your social life and family obligations?

If you drop 30 pounds will you still hang out with the same group of friends? Or will you become a different person? These are some of the things your loved ones probably will be thinking.

As you write your Action Plan you'll want to share your excitement with your friends and family. And that's great. Just don't be disappointed if all the responses are not positive. It's not that they don't wish you well. They are afraid to lose you.

This is not to say that no one will support your efforts. They will. My husband cooked dinner and cleaned the house so I could study when I went to grad school. And having his help and emotional support made getting my master's degree a little easier.

So enjoy the support you do get. And don't let negative reactions dampen your resolve or enthusiasm.

Putting It All Together

*You miss 100 percent of the shots
you never take.*

~ Wayne Gretzky

Over the next couple of weeks, take some time to carefully consider what you want. What are your long-term goals? Before you can create your plan you need to decide what you want as your end result.

Before you can set your short-term goals, you need to figure out what it will take to achieve your long-term objective. Study successful people. Look for those who are already where you want to be. Talk to a mentor.

To review, let's say your long-term goal is a "healthier lifestyle." Maybe this means becoming stronger and losing weight. Exercising regularly is one of your short-term goals. None of this is specific enough.

Start by clarifying your long-term goal. Instead of saying you want to be stronger and lose weight, plan to drop 10 pounds and be able to walk a 15-minute mile in two months. These are measurable goals. Rather than saying you will start to exercise, plan to exercise for 20 minutes three times a week, starting on Monday. This is something you can mark on your calendar, a visual reminder of your accomplishments. Begin today by taking the stairs instead of the elevator. Think how great you'll feel because you've taken action.

The same is true for your professional life. If you want to find new job or start your own business, you'll be more successful if you have a plan.

Let's say your long-term goal is to get another job. Your short-term goals may include reworking your resume, networking and looking for job openings. Break each of these down to relatively small, measurable tasks. For example, if you're sending out resumes, commit to sending out at least five each week. Just make sure the jobs are a good fit. Applying to any job that sounds interesting even if you're not qualified won't help you in the long run.

Begin working on your resume or making a list of job-search sites today. Ask your friends for help. If you need help from a professional ask for referrals. If your goal is to change careers, schedule some time this week for self-assessment and research. Plan to investigate at least one career that interests you each week.

What if your goal is to increase your business? Depending on your circumstances, signing on one new client a month may be a reasonable goal. You'll need to determine which daily and weekly actions will help you attract these new clients. Again, get advice from other businesspeople. Join an organization with a mentoring program.

Be careful not to push yourself too hard or too fast. While successful people know you have to stretch your talents to grow, they also know it's important to have reasonable expectations. Always be your own best friend. Never set yourself up for failure.

Remember my weight loss example. Knowing healthy weight loss means dropping one to two pounds a week trying to lose ten pounds in two weeks would be unrealistic. Keep this in mind when setting your business goals. Don't expect to find a new job or get six new clients in one month.

My college experience is a good example. As I mentioned, I was a college dropout. Since I left school before completing even the first semester, when I decided to return to college I had to start from scratch. Since I was on my own and working full-time I would have to go to school part-time in the evenings. The prospect of accumulating 120 credits was overwhelming. So I decided not to do it that way.

I started by taking two classes. After I completed four courses I matriculated into the University. But, I didn't begin working towards a bachelor's degree. I decided first to get my Associate's degree. If that went well I would continue. And I did.

Once I got my AA in Media Studies I decided to take a little break. By the following year, I was back pursuing my BA in English. Dividing my goal of obtaining a Bachelor's degree into two chunks made it seem more manageable to me. And that's what mattered. Because getting my two-year degree seemed achievable it was much easier for me. Eventually I went on to get a Master's in Applied Psychology.

Get started today by determining what you want. Be clear and concise. Next you're ready to develop your Action Plan. Start with your long-term goals. These are things you want to accomplish in at least six months to one year, or longer. Next, establish short-term goals. These include monthly, weekly and even daily targets that will move you toward your long-term objectives.

Once you've developed your Action Plan, don't let fear get in your way. Remember the only way to truly conquer your fears is to do whatever it is that you're afraid of. Having a plan to follow will help.

It's Ok to take it slow when you're starting something new. If you want to become a diver you don't jump off of the diving board before you learn to swim. You don't plan to ski down the expert trails your first weekend on the slopes.

You've already decided where you want to you. Your Action Plan is your route to get there. If you stay on track your destination will soon be in sight.

Are You Ready? Let's Go

It's never too late – in fiction or in life – to revise.

~ Nancy Thayer

Now that you have the basics you may be wondering when is the best time to get started. Many people set goals at the beginning of the year. These are often referred to as New Year's resolutions. By March these goals are mostly a memory.

Spring is another popular time for goal setting. One of the most popular goals is losing that "winter" weight in time for bathing-suit season. I've been guilty of that. And I'll bet you have too.

But the truth is that the right time is whenever it's the right time for you.

Did you see the movie *Julie & Julia*? It's a Nora Ephron film starring Meryl Streep and Amy Adams as Julia Child and Julie Powell, respectively. The story contrasts the life of Julia Child in the early years of her culinary career with the life of Julie Powell a young New Yorker who aspires to be a writer.

When the movie begins Powell is working in a call center by day and using cooking as an escape by night. At one point, feeling particularly dissatisfied with her life, Powell decides it's time to "do" something. She resolves to cook her way through Julia Child's *Mastering the Art of French Cooking* and blog about her experience. She creates the blog and titles it the Julie/Julia Project.

Julie Powell's project is a perfect example of a SMART goal in action.

Specific: Powell set a specific goal. Not, she would learn French cooking. She would cook her way through Julia Child's *Mastering the Art of French Cooking*.

Measurable: At the end of the project any one could measure her success. Either she cooked all the recipes in the book or she didn't. Easy.

Achievable: Powell's goal was to cook 524 recipes in 365 days, which was a little more than one recipe per day. For someone who already cooked, without the aid of processed food, every day it didn't sound unachievable.

Realistic: Powell already was a foodie. She prepared more than "basic" food every day. Coming home and baking from scratch was nothing out of the ordinary. So for her the goal was realistic. For me, who microwaves frozen vegetables, not so much.

Time-Framed: Finally, the project would last one year. Not just cook all the recipes in the book, but do it in one year. A point mentioned in the movie was that she was often guilty of not completing projects. Part of what kept her going when times got tough was the deadline.

For Powell the Julie/Julia Project was a huge success. Her blog was featured in a story in the *New York Times* and she came to the attention of journalists, agents and publishers. Not only did she master French cooking, she became a professional writer. *Julie & Julia* was the first major movie to be based on a blog.

While reaching your goals may not bring you fame or fortune they will bring you something priceless: the sense of accomplishment you get when you complete something that's important to you. Particularly when it's something you weren't sure you could do in the first place.

Whatever it is you want to do start by developing SMART goals. Make sure that you write them down. Studies have shown that people who actually write out their goals are more successful.

When is the right time to get started? The truth is there is no "right" time to set your goals. There is only the "right" time for you. Julie Powell started her project the day she was ready.

Is today that day for you?

Goals Worksheet

Goals Worksheet

Now you know how to set effective goals. Remember to use the SMART acronym. Make sure that your goals are:

Specific – is this something concrete?

Measurable – can it be measured by anyone?

Achievable – is this within my reach?

Realistic – do research and reason indicate this can be done?

Time Framed – is there a target date?

My long term goal – this is the main objective

_____

_____

_____

_____

My short-term goals – these will move me towards my main objective

_____

_____

_____

Monthly Goals:

1._____

2._____

3._____

(Make sure to include how you will measure your progress.)

Weekly Goals:

1._____

2._____

3._____

(Make sure to include how you will measure your progress.)

Daily Activities: These are things you will do on a daily basis that will help you move towards your long- and short-term goals. You might want to include activities such as positive thinking, reading, talking to your partner for support. Anything and everything that will help you move in the right direction.

1._____

2._____

3._____

Don't forget to plan rewards along the way.

www.ingramcontent.com/pod-product-compliance
Lightning Source LLC
Chambersburg PA
CBHW071021040426
42443CB00007B/879